*Martingale*®
& COMPANY

DAVE BRETHAUER

# Rubber Stamping with Watercolors

Rubber Stamping with Watercolors
© 2007 by Dave Brethauer

*Martingale* ®
& COMPANY

Martingale & Company
20205 144th Ave. NE
Woodinville, WA 98072-8478 USA
www.martingale-pub.com

Projects originally appeared in *Stamp in Color: Techniques for Enhancing Your Artwork* by Dave Brethauer, published by Martingale & Company in 2000.

## CREDITS

President & CEO ~ Tom Wierzbicki
Publisher ~ Jane Hamada
Editorial Director ~ Mary V. Green
Managing Editor ~ Tina Cook
Technical Editor ~ Candie Frankel
Copy Editor ~ Miriam Bulmer
Design Director ~ Stan Green
Assistant Design Director ~ Regina Girard
Illustrator ~ Laurel Strand
Cover & Text Designer ~ Stan Green
Photographer ~ Brent Kane

Printed in China
12 11 10 09 08 07     8 7 6 5 4 3 2 1

ISBN: 978-1-56477-831-4

## MISSION STATEMENT
Dedicated to providing quality products and service to inspire creativity.

# Contents

# Working with Watercolors

There is nothing quite like the look of watercolor. A perfect wash of color across a sky or a smooth blend over the surface of a leaf can make a person do a double take. Even the word *watercolor* is romantic. But watercolor techniques can be elusive. They involve planning and timing but also stepping back and letting the paint do more or less its own thing. It is hard to control these watery paints, but often you don't want to—their unpredictable nature is also their allure. In this section, you will learn about the tools, materials, and techniques required to start making your own watercolor magic.

## Tools and Materials

### BRUSHES

Despite the wide variety of brushes available, choosing the right one for your project is relatively easy, once you know the basics. Brushes come in different types, shapes, and sizes. Which brush you choose depends on the size of your project and the techniques you want to use when painting.

### Brush Types

Paintbrushes are made either with synthetic fibers, such as nylon, or with natural fibers, such as animal hairs. Synthetic brushes are the less expensive of the two, and they do perform well, especially for small projects. However, you may find you prefer a natural-fiber brush. Natural bristles are soft and flexible. They lay down the paint smoothly and they also seem to hold more paint, letting you color larger areas before reloading.

### Brush Shapes

Paintbrushes are designed in different shapes for different jobs. Round brushes are the most effective for painting small detailed areas. Flat brushes are excellent for filling in large areas with a wash of color. The shape of the brush can also affect how much paint can be loaded into the bristles.

### Brush Sizes

Keep in mind the area you will be painting when choosing a paintbrush size. For card-size projects, I recommend a No. 4 or No. 6 round brush. These sizes will allow you to paint small areas in a stamped image accurately. For more expansive areas, you may find a larger round brush more efficient, particularly if you are a beginner. Occasionally I will use a 1" flat brush to surround a stamped image with color. In watercolor painting, the faster you paint an area, the more even the color will appear when dry.

### Brush Care

Avoid letting your brushes stand in a cup of water for extended periods of time. When you finish painting, rinse your brush in clear water, pull the bristles to a point, and lay the brush flat to dry. Stand dry brushes upright in a container so the bristles aren't pressing against anything.

## WATERCOLOR PAPER

Watercolor paper is thick and richly textured. The paint finds its way into the thousands of dimples across the paper surface in such a way that both the paper and the color appear richer and more intense. Watercolor paper can be purchased in blocks, in tablets, or as individual sheets.

### Watercolor Blocks

A watercolor block is a stack of watercolor papers glued together on all four sides. You stamp and paint on the top sheet while it is still attached. The paint will not leak through to the next sheet, and the glued sides keep the paper flat so that you don't need to worry about curling as you add water to the surface. When your finished work is dry, simply insert a brush handle or butter knife into the small unglued opening on the block to peel off the top layer.

*The sealed edges of a watercolor block help the paper remain flat during painting.*

## Watercolor Tablets and Sheets

Sheets of watercolor paper, both machine-made and handmade papers, can be purchased in tablet form or individually. You can choose either. Since the edges are not fixed in place, as they are in a block, it is possible for some curling to occur during painting. On small projects this curling tends to be minimal, but if you are painting a large area with copious amounts of paint and water you may want to stretch your sheet first. Soak the sheet in room-temperature water for a few minutes, then lay it out on a smooth, flat work surface. Soak up the excess water with a sponge and then smooth out the paper with your hand. Secure all four edges with tape or pushpins so that the sheet will remain flat as it dries. Once the sheet is dry, you can begin working on it without having the edges curl.

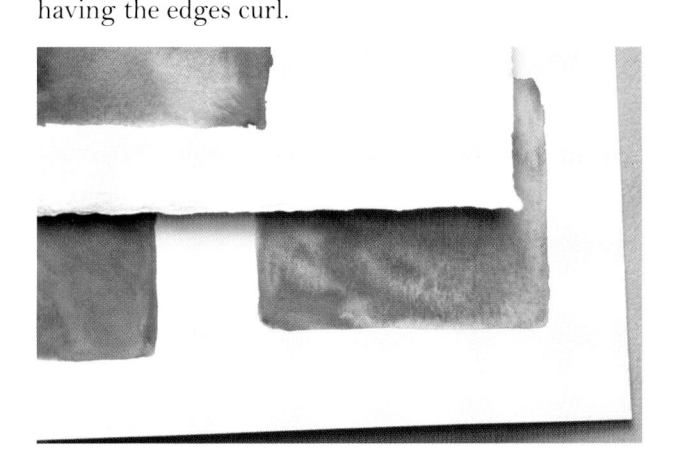

*Handmade (top) and machine-made sheets.*

## Paper Weights and Surfaces

Examine a sheet of watercolor paper and you will see that it is made to absorb a lot of liquid. I use 140-lb. paper, a common machine-made paper weight, for most of my projects. A paper's weight refers to the density of its fibers; the heavier the weight, the thicker the paper. Keep in mind, though, that weight is not always an accurate indicator of a handmade paper's thickness because of the variations inherent in any given sheet.

A paper's surface feel depends on whether it was manufactured using a hot-press method (for a smooth surface) or a cold-press method (for a textured surface). Smooth hot-press watercolor papers are used for illustration techniques such as pen-and-ink drawings that are then colored with watercolor. For coloring in stamped images, I prefer the texture of cold-press papers. The microscopic jags and valleys on the surface give the paper some tooth so that the paint has something to hold on to. Textured paper seems to make the painting process more forgiving. For a rougher texture yet, you can experiment with handmade watercolor papers.

## WATERCOLOR PAINTS

The gorgeous tones and shading associated with watercolors are the result of complex paint pigments. So many different shades are available that the selection may at first seem overwhelming. As a beginner you will need only a few basic colors, but once you acquire a feel for what shades work well together you may find yourself desiring a greener blue or a red with more orange in it. As you progress, you will discover which colors you are naturally drawn to and also how to mix, blend, and create washes to achieve a virtually endless range of shades.

### Choosing Your Paints

Watercolor pigment is sold in dry solid blocks or wet in tubes. Dry paints can be challenging to work with. They need to be wetted quite often, and trying to lift up paint that is not sufficiently moist can be hard on your paintbrush.

Still, dry pigments are convenient and are often preferable for travel because of their compact, portable nature.

The paint pigment sold in tubes is concentrated and must be extended with water in order to be

## Understanding Paint Colors

Choosing and mixing the colors you will use in your projects is sometimes more fun than the painting itself. A simple color chart that you paint yourself will help you develop your own sense of what combinations work well.

A key concept to remember is that there is no "true" red, "true" blue, or "true" yellow with

*Watercolor palettes come in a variety of shapes and sizes, as shown below.*

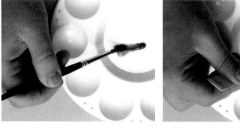

*Add a squirt of tube paint to the palette and then add water off to the side of the paint. To make the color paler, add water. To make the color stronger, pull in more paint.*

usable. Although tube watercolors may seem intim-idating at first, I recommend them because they blend easily and the colors are fabulous. To use the paint, simply squeeze a small amount onto a palette (I use a dinner plate) and mix in a few drops of water using your paintbrush. The more water you add, the paler the color. Several different colors can be deposited around the edge of the plate, with plenty of room left in the middle for mixing. This approach can become messy and requires planning to avoid waste. Paint that has dried on the plate can be reconstituted, but the results are unpredictable and the paint may not mix evenly.

## Easy Watercolor Techniques

Water is obviously an element in all watercolor techniques. If you're just getting acquainted with watercolors, begin by brushing the surface of the paper liberally with plain water. This prewetting ensures that the paint will achieve full, smooth, even coverage and that it won't dry prematurely, leaving

*When mixing analogous hues, choose colors that are close to one another on the color wheel for a bright shade and hues that are farther apart for a muted shade. Here, cadmium red + cadmium yellow = brilliant orange, while alizarin crimson + lemon yellow = muted orange.*

watercolor paints. The color red, for instance, might be cadmium red, which is an orange-red, or alizarin crimson, a violet-red. Understanding that the red you use may be more orange or more violet will allow you to create a mix that produces precisely the shade you are looking for. For example, in some projects you may want a muted orange and in others you may want a brilliant orange. Knowing how to obtain these shades is easy once you understand the color bias already present in the paints.

behind paint lines or brush marks. Over time, as you develop your skills and learn how to paint quickly, prewetting will become optional and you can just jump right into a project.

Water also helps you control the color saturation. For lighter, softer, more transparent color, use more water. For stronger, more intense color, use less water and more paint. This principle becomes especially relevant when you begin blending colors on paper.

*The same color diluted with light, moderate, and generous amounts of water.*

The amount of water in a paint mixture also affects how it interacts with other paint mixtures. If one mix has more water than another, the more diluted mix will push the less diluted color out of the way.

*A mixture with more water will push its way into a neighboring color. The results are wonderfully unpredictable.*

**TIP** *Putting a drop of paint into a wet area is a fun, unpredictable technique. Once dry, the color will be strongest where it was initially deposited and show a gradual fade from this spot.*

## WASHES

A wash—the technique most often associated with watercolor—is a perfect, flowing gradation of color across an area. A wash may involve only one color that fades from dark to light, or it may feature a combination of colors—for example, green into blue into purple. The ability of this fluid medium to gradually shift through the colors of the spectrum is amazing.

### Painting a Watercolor Wash

1. Determine the area you want the wash to fill. Prewet this area by brushing it with plain water. The surface should be slightly wet, so that you can see a sheen.

2. Squeeze some paint onto your palette, enough to fill the wash area (you don't want to run out of paint midway). Mix the paint with your brush, adding a little water to make it spreadable.

3. Touch a corner of the prewetted area with the loaded brush. You will observe the paint spreading into the wet area on its own.

4. Slowly brush the paint across the prewetted area, keeping the tip of the brush on the paper as much as possible. To avoid dried paint lines, work into the paint edge while it is still wet.

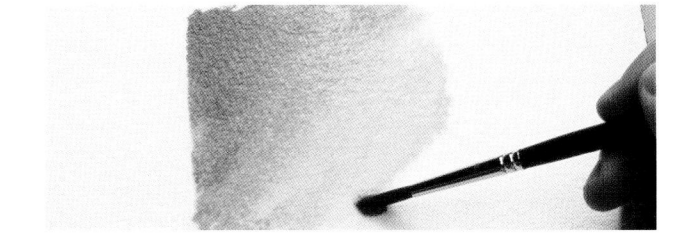

5.  When your brush runs out of paint, pull it to the edge of the wet area and lift it off the paper. (Removing the brush in the middle will create a noticeable drop of color at that spot.) Reload the brush with paint and continue, starting inside the painted area and working toward your endpoint.

6.  A successful wash will show a gradual change of color across the area. The color may fade out or randomly brighten and soften.

**TIP** *The colors in a wash lighten as they dry. If your wash looks a little stronger or darker when wet than you intended, then you're doing it correctly.*

## BLENDING

Blending is a watercolor skill that yields spectacular results, simultaneously adding color interest and depth. The goal is to lay down two or more colors and then mix them together so that they create new in-between colors that flow seamlessly, one into another.

Painting the initial color areas is relatively easy, but creating a flawless blend takes practice. It is essential to use enough liquid, so that the area connecting two colors does not stand out. Start with similar paint-to-water ratios for each color. As your blending skills increase, you can try varying the ratios for more interesting and unexpected results. A more watery mixture, remember, will push an adjacent color out of the way.

### Blending Watercolors

1.  Select the colors you want to blend. Squeeze equal amounts of each onto your palette, and add equal amounts of water to each for a spreadable consistency.

2.  Define the area you will paint by prewetting the area with plain water.

3.  Visually divide the area into sections, one for each color. Starting at one corner, begin applying the lightest color to the first of the sections.

4.  Dip your brush, without rinsing, into the second color on your palette. Begin painting the second section. Drag this color a little bit into the first section's color to encourage their mixing.

5.  Dip your brush, again without rinsing, into the third color and paint the third section. Drag the second and third colors together, keeping the brush on the paper.

**TIP** *For more control over the color mix, rinse the brush between each color. If the colors aren't blending at all, then the paint is drying out too quickly. Try working faster, or use more paint on your brush.*

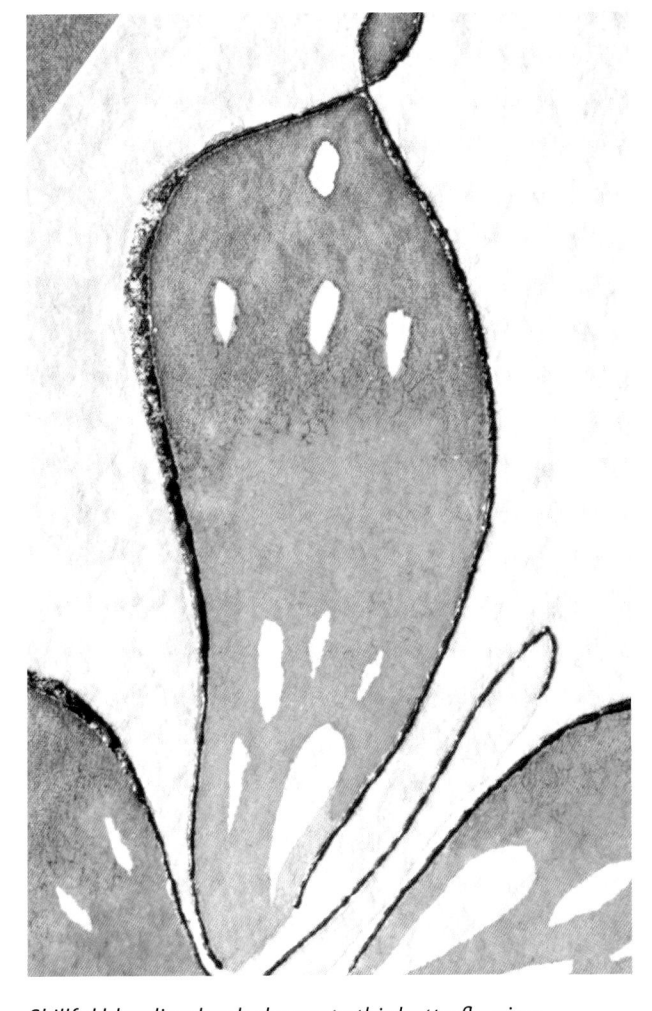

*Skillful blending lends drama to this butterfly wing.*

## LAYERING COLOR

Another aspect of watercolor pigments is their transparency/opacity. There are four basic gradations—transparent, semitransparent, semi-opaque, and opaque—with some hues being more "see-through" than others. Layering one of the more transparent colors over a base coat can produce exciting new colors. For instance, when you paint Windsor blue over a dry underlayer of lemon yellow, the result is a complex shade of blue with rich yellow undertones. Unlike mixing, in which two hues are combined to make a third hue (for example, yellow + blue = green), layering is a way

of "influencing" a color by allowing another color to show through it. The effect is subtle and mysterious.

*Layered colors*

### Layering Watercolors

1. Paint the selected area in a solid color, such as cadmium yellow. Since you want a solid underlayer, no prewetting is required.

2. Let the paint dry completely, preferably overnight.

3. Paint a wash of cadmium red over the cadmium yellow. Try to make one end a strong red and slowly fade out the color as you move across. (See "Painting a Watercolor Wash," page 7.)

   Note how the underpainted and plain cadmium reds differ. Also note how the yellow shows up more and more as the cadmium red wash fades.

## ERASING MISTAKES

I have always felt that there's no such thing as a mistake when you paint a project. If, however, you feel the need to remove a stray brushstroke or two, here's a technique you can use. It's best to act quickly, while the paint is still wet.

### Removing Watercolor Paint

1. Rinse your brush and squeeze out the excess water.

2. Touch your brush to the stray mark and soak up the paint. Repeat steps 1 and 2 as needed.

3. If the brush is not successful in picking up any of the color, the paint has probably dried. Carefully rewet the area with plain water, then repeat steps 1 and 2.

# Baby Carriage

*One way of adding extra depth is to fill the entire piece of watercolor paper with color. In this card, a purply blue wash helps set off and highlight the pink carriage. This technique is especially effective when you want to make a plain white background appear less stark.*

*Finished size: 4¼" x 5½"*

## Materials

Sky blue note card,
  4¼" x 5½" (folded size)

Handmade Rose card stock,
  3¾" x 4"

Watercolor paper, about 5" x 5½"

Baby Carriage rubber stamp

Midnight pigment inkpad

Clear embossing powder

Cotman watercolors:
    Permanent Rose
    Lemon Yellow
    Cobalt Blue
Designer Gouache Zinc White

Double-coated tape

**TIP** *Adding a little white gouache to your watercolor mix makes the paint more opaque and improves the viscosity. Try a gouache mix over a prewetted area when you want smooth, even color coverage.*

## Instructions

1. Stamp the baby carriage onto watercolor paper using midnight pigment ink. Sprinkle clear embossing powder on the wet ink and shake off the excess. Heat with a heating tool to melt the powder.

2. Prewet a 3" x 3" area around the carriage. Tint the water slightly, if necessary, to make the wet area easier to see.

3. Mix the permanent rose and cobalt blue watercolors with white gouache to create a soft lavender. Paint the prewetted area, filling it in solidly with color.

4. Dilute permanent rose paint with water to make a soft pink color. Prewet the carriage body, hood, and wheels, and paint them pink.

5. Paint the button at the base of the hood lemon yellow.

6. Trim the baby carriage piece to 3¼" x 3½". Using double-coated tape, mount the baby carriage piece on the rose card stock. Mount the rose card stock on the note card.

*Try these alternative color schemes to create an entirely different look.*

*Emerald, Lemon Yellow, and Permanent Rose*

*Permanent Rose and Cadmium Yellow*

*Permanent Rose and Cobalt Blue*

# House on a Hill

This card uses watercolor blending to achieve a playful lighting effect. Colors are applied at opposite ends of each shape in the stamped image and then pulled together to create brand-new middle color. A smooth blend is crucial for this dazzling effect and can be achieved by using plenty of paint and keeping the area wet as you fill in. Note how the analogous yellow/green/blue background makes the purple house at the center pop out.

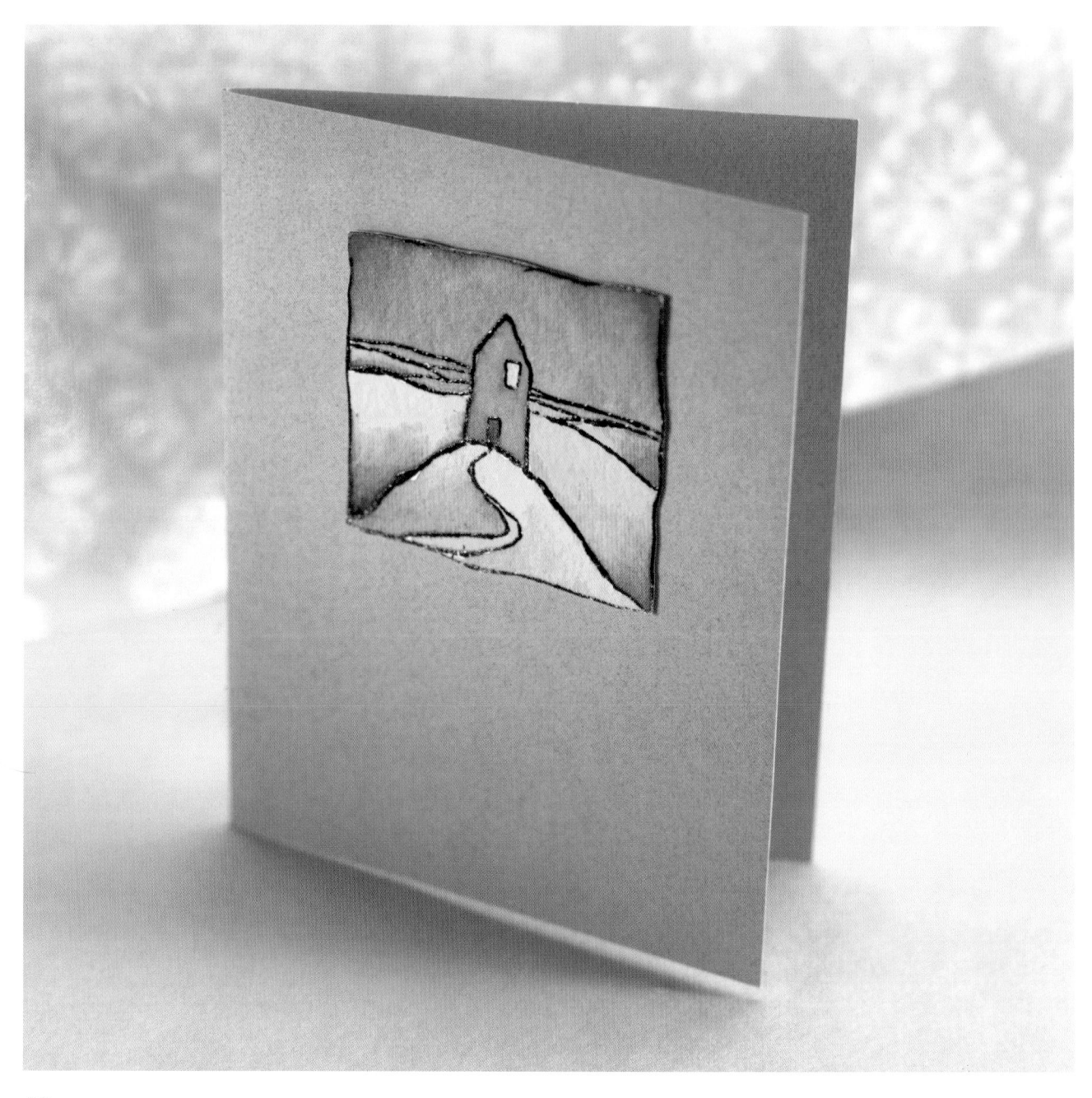

Finished size: 4¼" x 5½"

## Materials

Lavender note card, 4¼" x 5½"
(folded size)

Watercolor paper, about 4" x 4"

House on a Hill rubber stamp

Black pigment inkpad

Clear embossing powder

Cotman watercolors:
Cobalt Blue
Turquoise
Permanent Rose
Lemon Yellow
Intense Green
Sap Green

Double-coated tape

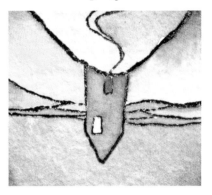

Step 5

TIP *To avoid spotting and
streaking on dry paper, work
quickly while the paint is still wet.*

## Instructions

1. Stamp the house on a hill image onto watercolor paper using black pigment ink. Sprinkle clear embossing powder on the wet ink and shake off the excess. Heat with a heating tool to melt the powder.

2. Squeeze some lemon yellow paint onto a palette. Mix in a drop or two of water—just enough to make the paint spreadable without diluting the color. Paint the two large side hills on each side of the house, starting at the top and stopping about three-quarters of the way down.

3. Paint the remainder of each large hill using a mix of cobalt blue and sap green. This green mixture will overpower the yellow, so apply it sparingly and don't pull the green into the yellow area too far; just do a little cautious mixing where the yellow and green meet. If you are using enough liquid, the paint will do most of the work for you. (See "Blending Watercolors," page 8.)

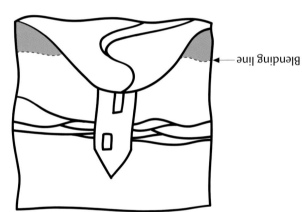

Step 3

← Blending line

4. Paint the remaining distant hills lemon yellow. Add a drop of the green mixture to the bottom or side edge of each outlined area. Let the green and yellow paints run together.

5. Squeeze some cobalt blue paint onto a palette and dilute with water, as in step 2. Paint the upper right and left corners of the sky, drawing the blue color about halfway to the house. Paint the remainder of the sky using a mix of turquoise and intense green, and draw it into the cobalt blue areas.

6. Mix the sap green and lemon yellow watercolors to make chartreuse. Paint the hill in the foreground from left to right, adding more water to the mix as you go to lighten the color.

7. Mix permanent rose and cobalt blue to make purple. Paint the house purple. Paint the door cobalt blue. Paint the window and the path lemon yellow. Let dry.

8. Cut out the scene as close as possible to the embossed outline. Using double-coated tape, mount the cutout on the note card.

# Quickly Butterfly

O nce you have acquired some skill at blending, you are ready to add more depth to your painting. In the previous projects, the colors were all applied directly over a white background. In this exercise, you will see how layering one color over another can add richness and complexity to your image. First, you will paint an underlayer of yellow, then you will paint over it with a blend of blues and greens. The underlayer will show through where the second layer wasn't painted, brightening the entire image.

*Finished size: 5¼" x 5¼"*

# Materials

Lavender card stock, 10½" x 5¼"

Denim card stock, 4" x 4"

Watercolor paper, about 5½" x 5½"

Four ⅛" baby blue eyelets

Swirly Butterfly rubber stamp

Black pigment inkpad

Clear embossing powder

Cotman watercolors:
    Cadmium Yellow Light
    Intense Green
    Turquoise

Double-coated tape

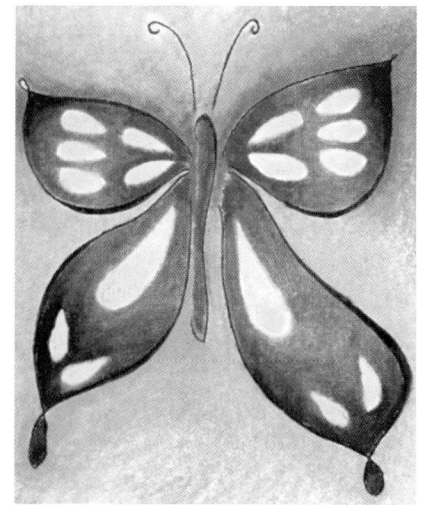

*As an alternative, colored pencils allow you to add lots of color with greater control.*

# Instructions

1. Stamp the swirly butterfly onto watercolor paper using black pigment ink. Sprinkle clear embossing powder on the wet ink, and shake off the excess. Heat with a heating tool to melt the powder.

2. See "Layering Watercolors," page 9. For the underpainted layer, paint the butterfly wings and the body cadmium yellow. Let dry overnight.

3. Prewet the 4½"-square area surrounding the butterfly with water. Dilute turquoise paint with water to create a pale aqua color. Paint the wet area around the butterfly. Let dry 1 hour.

4. For the top layer, mix the cadmium yellow and intense green watercolors to create a grassy green color. Brush this green color onto a butterfly wing, starting from the body and working out about halfway; as you work, leave some areas open to create a yellow spotted pattern. Rinse the brush and squeeze out the excess water (shown below left).

5. Apply turquoise paint to the other end of the wing in the same way. Paint toward the green paint until the two colors touch. If the two paints are very wet, simply let them mingle by themselves to create an interesting edge pattern. If they don't mingle on their own, swirl the touching edges slightly with the tip of your brush to help the paints flow together (shown below right).

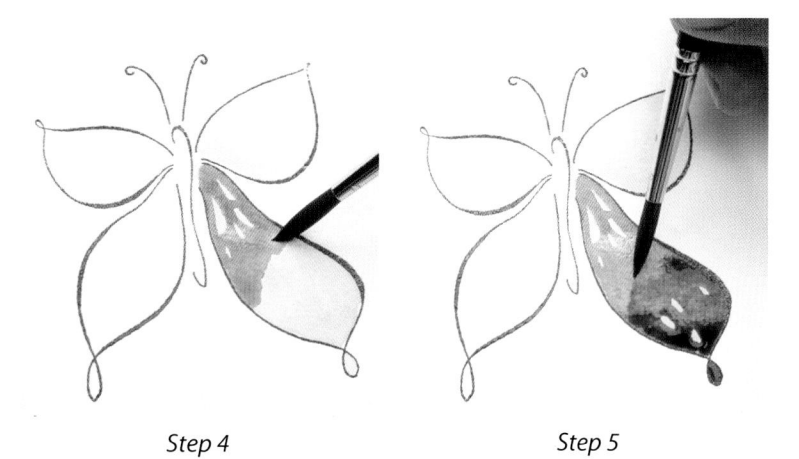

*Step 4*                    *Step 5*

6. Repeat steps 4 and 5 for each butterfly wing. Let dry.

7. Trim the butterfly piece to 3½" x 3½". Fold the lavender card stock in half to make a 5¼" x 5¼" card. Open the card and lay it flat. Using double-coated tape, mount the butterfly piece on the denim card stock. Mount the denim card stock on the lavender card. At each corner of the denim square, punch a ⅛" hole and install a baby blue eyelet.

#  Bunny

*This is a wonderful card to help you learn how to put "suggestive" elements in a painting. The background is a quick splash of blue for the sky and a bit of green for the hill. Those two elements come together to create a whole scene. The beauty of this technique is its speed. The blue is literally laid down with just a few brushstrokes, for the feel of sky peeking through the clouds. Paint the green mound and instantly you have a platform for two bunnies!*

*Finished size: 4¼" x 5½"*

## Materials

Moonbeam note card, 4¼" x 5½"
(folded size)

Aqua card stock, 3½" square

White laid card stock, about 5" square

Watercolor paper, about 3" square

Four Bunnies in a Row rubber stamp

Black pigment inkpad

Clear embossing powder

Cotman watercolors:
    Cobalt Blue
    Rose Madder
    Sap Green

Foam mounting tape

Double-coated tape

*Step 5*

# Instructions

1. Using black pigment ink, ink two of the four bunnies on the stamp. Stamp the inked image onto watercolor paper. Sprinkle clear embossing powder on the wet ink and shake off the excess. Heat with a heating tool to melt the powder.

2. Dilute cobalt blue with water to create a pale blue color. Paint just inside the right edge of the bunny bodies, heads, and ears to suggest shadows.

3. Paint a dot of rose madder onto the bunny noses. Set aside to dry.

4. Lightly pencil in a 3¾" box on the white laid card stock. For the sky, paint a few loose strokes of cobalt blue across the upper two-thirds of the box. Rinse the brush and squeeze out the excess water. For the hillside, paint a green dome shape across the lower third.

*Step 4*

5. When the bunny pair is thoroughly dry, cut it out using an X-Acto knife. Using foam tape, mount the bunnies on the painted card stock, as if they were sitting on the hillside. Trim this scene to 3¼" x 3¼" so the bunnies are centered. Using double-coated tape, mount the bunny scene on the aqua card stock. Mount the aqua card stock on the moonbeam note card.

# Teacup Quattro

$S$imple repetition turns a single stamped image into a lively display of dancing teacups. Dark and light colors play off one another here. The red saucers, painted so thickly as to be nearly opaque, are handsomely set off by the surrounding light ochre wash. Note the absence of color inside the teacups, which adds to the drama. By leaving parts of a design blank and allowing the white paper to show through, you add bright highlights to your composition.

*Finished size: 5½" x 8½"*

## Materials

Vanilla card stock, 11" x 8½"

Nutmeg card stock, 4⅝" x 4"

Watercolor paper, about 6½" x 6"

Teacup rubber stamp

Black pigment inkpad

Clear embossing powder

Cotman watercolors:
    Yellow Ochre
    Indian Red
    Cadmium Red Deep Hue

Double-coated tape

**TIP** *Drag your brush along the area you want to lighten.*

*The brush absorbs excess paint.*

## Instructions

1. Stamp 4 teacups onto watercolor paper using black pigment ink; arrange the cups in a closely spaced grid, tilting each image slightly so the design is not static. Sprinkle clear embossing powder on the wet ink and shake off the excess. Heat with a heating tool to melt the powder.

2. Prewet the area around the teacups. Dilute yellow ochre paint with water to make a light wash. Fill in the background, allowing for heavier color saturation in some areas. (See "Painting a Watercolor Wash," page 7.) Let dry.

3. For each saucer, mix Indian red and a little cadmium red, using as little water as possible. Paint the saucer from one end to the other, adding more cadmium red as you go to produce a gradual brightening of the color.

4. For each teacup, mix yellow ochre and a touch of Indian red to make a butterscotch color. Brush this mix along the right edge of the cup. Fill in the area from right to left, adding water to the mix as you go to lighten the color. Leave the inside of the cups white. Let dry.

5. Trim the teacup piece to 4⅜" x 3¾". Fold the vanilla card stock in half to make a 5½" x 8½" card. Using double-coated tape, mount the teacup piece on the nutmeg card stock, then mount both on the vanilla card.

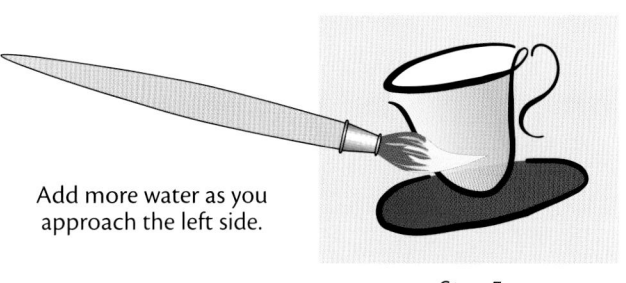

Add more water as you approach the left side.

*Step 5*

**TIP** *If the area you just painted appears too solid, you can fix it as long as the paint is still wet. Rinse your brush, squeeze out the excess water, then drag the brush along the side you wish to lighten, as shown at right. The brush will soak up the excess paint, lightening the area. Because the surrounding paint will try to fill the new lightened area, you may have to repeat this procedure several times.*

# Christmas Present

*T*his red package gets its golden yellow halo from wet-on-wet blending, a technique that creates very fluid color changes. The paper is prewetted twice, first with plain water and then with yellow watercolor. Green watercolor is then pulled into the yellow area. The result is a smooth halo of color around the central image.

*Finished size: 5½" x 4¼"*

## Materials

Crimson card stock, 11" x 4¼"

Gold metallic card stock, 4¾" x 3"

Watercolor paper, about 6½" x 5"

Present rubber stamp

Gold embossing powder

Gold pigment inkpad

Cotman watercolors:
Lemon Yellow
Sap Green
Indian Red
Cadmium Red Deep Hue

Double-coated tape

## Instructions

1.  Stamp a present onto the watercolor paper using gold pigment ink. Sprinkle gold embossing powder on the wet ink and shake off the excess. Heat with a heating tool to melt the powder.

2.  Prewet the area around the present with plain water. Working quickly, while the paper is still very wet, brush lemon yellow paint around the package, working out about 1" in all directions. (See "Painting a Watercolor Wash," page 7.) Do not rinse the brush.

3.  Make sure the paper is still damp, and rewet if necessary. Paint the corners of the paper sap green. Pull the green partway into the yellow, stopping about ¼" from the present so a yellow halo remains around it. (See photo below and "Blending Watercolors," page 8.)

*Step 3*

4.  Paint the left plane surface of the present Indian red. Paint the front cadmium red. Paint the top a mix of Indian red and cadmium red. Let dry.

5.  Trim the Christmas present piece to 4¾" x 2½". Fold the crimson card in half to make a 5½" x 4¼" note card. Using double-coated tape, mount the Christmas present piece on the gold metallic card stock, then mount both on the crimson note card.

# Four Snowmen and Star

When watercolors are still wet on the paper, they can be manipulated in various ways. If a color is too strong, a dry brush can soak up the excess. If two different colors meet, they will naturally intermingle to create interesting edge patterns. One characteristic behavior is that plain water, when added to wet color, will push the standing pigment out of the way. In this card, letting a single drop of water fall on the star pushes away the blue background color and creates a white halo. Results with this technique are difficult to control—they are a factor of the paper surface, the amount of water, and so forth—but you can experiment. Just remember to add the water while the paint is still wet.

*Finished size: 5½" x 4¼"*

## Materials

Navy note card, 5½" x 4¼" (folded size)

Watercolor paper, about 5½" x 4"

Four Snowmen and Star rubber stamp

Black pigment inkpad

Clear embossing powder

Cotman watercolors:
Cadmium Red Deep Hue
Lemon Yellow
Sap Green
Cobalt Blue
Permanent Rose

Double-coated tape

**TIP** *Embossed images are extra easy to paint with watercolors. The raised lines keep the wet areas from bleeding into each other*

## Instructions

1. Stamp the snowmen onto watercolor paper using black pigment ink. Sprinkle clear embossing powder on the wet ink and shake off the excess. Heat with a heating tool to melt the powder.

2. Prewet the sky area behind the snowmen. Using cobalt blue watercolor, paint across the wet area from corner to corner, right up to the star outline. Add a touch of permanent rose here and there and mix it in to create purple tones.

3. While the background is still wet, rinse your brush. Let a single drop of clear water fall on the star. The water will push the blue paint away from the star, creating a bright halo. The size of the halo will depend on the amount of water used.

4. Paint the scarves and hats cadmium red, cadmium yellow, sap green, orange (cadmium red plus cadmium yellow), and light green (sap green plus cadmium yellow).

5. Paint the star cadmium yellow. Let dry.

6. Cut out the snowmen on the embossed outline. Using double-coated tape, mount the snowmen on the navy note card.

Step 2

Step 3

# More Ideas

BABY ANNOUNCEMENT: *Sweet and simple, this uncluttered layout calls for just a few touches of watercolor. No blending is involved, but the colors still look lovely under their vellum overlay.*

SINGLE SNOWMAN CARD: *It's easy to create an entire landscape around a single stamped image. Just paint in the sky and the white hillside emerges from the negative space.*

FIVE-PETALED FLOWER CARD: *This bright card uses relatively small amounts of water, for strong, intense colors.*

FLOWER WREATH CARD: *For this card, one stamp was used to produce six watercolor cutouts. When mounted together in a circle on the card, these rose cutouts form a lovely floral wreath.*

POTTED FLOWER CARD: *The soft yellow watercolor background, pale red and orange pot, and light green leaves form an understated backdrop for the stronger red flower petals.*

BUTTERFLY CARD: *The flow of watercolor creates a cheery halo around the butterfly and provides a soft backdrop to the bright "confetti" droplets added at the end.*